AF228544

FOSSILS, ROCKS, AND MINERALS

Marcia Amidon Lusted

Abdo Reference

An Imprint of Abdo Publishing | abdobooks.com

CONTENTS

Choose any location in the world, and chances are good that there will be fossils, rocks, or minerals there. These objects form in different ways and have distinct characteristics. Fossils, rocks, and minerals can tell people how Earth formed, how it has changed, and the plants and animals that once inhabited it.

WHAT ARE MINERALS?

A mineral is an inorganic substance, meaning that it is not alive. There are more than 5,000 types of minerals on Earth. All minerals have certain features:

- All minerals occur naturally. They are not created by people.

- All minerals are solid.

- A mineral has a crystal structure. This is an orderly, symmetrical, and repeating arrangement of atoms.

- Every mineral has a set chemical composition. That means a mineral is always made up of the same elements. Sometimes it will just have one element.

WHAT ARE ROCKS?

Rocks are made up of minerals. They can appear in many different shapes and sizes. Some rocks may contain pieces of organic matter. Rocks can be classified in three ways, depending on how they formed. Rocks are either igneous, sedimentary, or metamorphic.

- Igneous rocks are created when molten magma or lava solidifies.

- Sedimentary rocks are formed by deposits of dead plants and sediments, which can include sand and silt.

- Metamorphic rocks are created when rocks underground are changed by heat or pressure.

Rocks have two things in common with minerals. First, both rocks and minerals are found in Earth's outer crust. Second, people view some rocks and minerals as valuable because they can be used in manufacturing or construction. Sometimes people extract useful minerals from rocks.

WHAT ARE FOSSILS?

Fossils are often found in sedimentary rocks. They are the remains of animals and plants. Over time, the remains are sometimes replaced with minerals.

Fossils preserve pieces of organisms, such as shells, feathers, leaves, or bones. Most living things decompose quickly after they die, and only a small number are preserved as fossils. Some experts think that only one bone in a billion ends up becoming a fossil. In addition, fossils must be at least 10,000 years old to be classified as such. Fossils often take on the color of the rock they are preserved in.

Geologic Time Scale

	Name	Date
Period	Cambrian	541 to 485.4 million years ago
Period	Ordovician	485.4 to 443.8 million years ago
Period	Silurian	443.8 to 419.2 million years ago
Period	Devonian	419.2 to 358.9 million years ago
Period	Carboniferous	358.9 to 298.9 million years ago
Period	Permian	298.9 to 251.9 million years ago
Period	Triassic	251.9 to 201.3 million years ago
Period	Jurassic	201.3 to 145 million years ago
Period	Cretaceous	145 to 66 million years ago
Epoch	Paleocene	66 to 56 million years ago
Epoch	Eocene	56 to 33.9 million years ago
Epoch	Oligocene	33.9 to 23 million years ago
Epoch	Miocene	23 to 5.3 million years ago
Epoch	Pliocene	5.3 to 2.6 million years ago
Epoch	Pleistocene	2.6 million years ago to 11,700 years ago
Epoch	Holocene	11,700 years ago to the present day

HOW TO USE THIS BOOK

INVERTEBRATE FOSSILS

SAND DOLLAR *(ENCOPE)*

Sand dollars have been around since the Miocene epoch. They bury themselves in the sand in warm, shallow waters. These animals have rigid skeletons. They are very flat and thin with slightly domed tops. Sand dollars have flower-like patterns on their tops. The edges of these animals have slits. Living sand dollars are deep brown or purplish red. When fossilized, sand dollars can be brown or white.

HOW TO SPOT

Size: 3.5 inches (8.9 cm) long

Identifying Features: Round with flower-like patterns

Range: North and South America

Habitat: Warm, shallow waters

FUN FACT

Sand dollars got their name because sometimes their remains are silvery white and look like silver dollars.

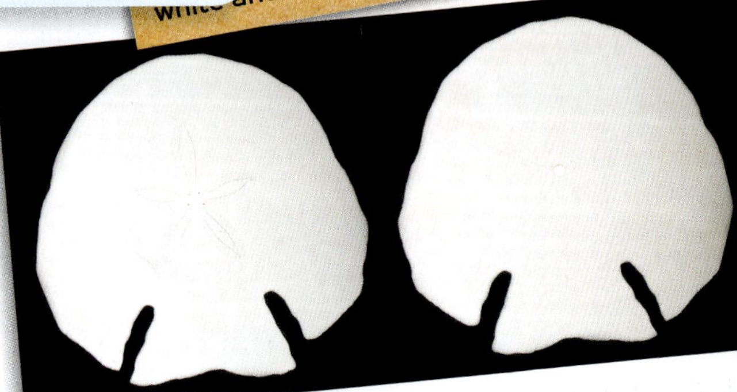

14

6

The genus name appears here.

CALLOP *(PECTEN)*

scallop has two shells connected by a ligament. The shells
ve broad ribs that start at the base and spread upward.
callops have been around since the Late Eocene epoch.
hey are found all over the world. These animals prefer to
ve in clean sands and fairly shallow waters. They often
g depressions in seabed sands and rest in them. Scallop
ossils are usually just the shells. The ligament connecting
he shells is rarely preserved.

This paragraph tells readers about the topic.

HOW TO SPOT

Size: 3.1 inches (7.9 cm) long
Identifying Features: Ribbed shell
Range: Worldwide
Habitat: Clean sands and shallow waters

In the fossil entries, Range and Habitat refer to where the genus lived while alive.

FUN FACT

Scallops can swim by opening and closing their hinged shells.

Fun Facts give interesting information related to the topic.

GETTING PRESERVED

For something to be preserved as a fossil, it needs to
meet certain conditions that stop the decaying process.
For instance, the organism needs to be protected
from water and air. Many fossils are found in marine or
fresh water sediments. In these environments, the animals
were buried in oxygen-deprived clay or silt. They were able
to form into fossils.

15

Sidebars provide additional information about the topic.

DRAGONFLY *(PETALURA)*

Petalura is a genus of dragonfly. This creature has lived on Earth since the Jurassic period. A dragonfly has two forewings and two hindwings. It also has a long, slender tail. These features may be seen in fossils. The *Petalura* fossil forms when the dragonfly dies in a watery environment and is then buried in silt or clay. The sediment hardens into rock. Then, the decaying dragonfly leaves behind its imprint in the rock.

HOW TO SPOT

Size: 1.25 inches (3 cm) long

Identifying Features: A distinct dragonfly shape with four broad, veined wings

Range: Europe, Australia, New Zealand, and islands in the South Pacific Ocean

Habitat: Near fresh water

FUN FACT

Insect fossils from the Early Devonian period don't have wings. It's not until the Late Carboniferous period that many of them were able to fly.

WHERE ARE FOSSILS FOUND?

Fossils are usually found in sedimentary rocks. People can find fossils in cliffs and other exposed areas near coasts. They can also find fossils in quarries, in arid areas such as deserts, and in rugged terrain with layered rocks.

GIANT CERITH *(CAMPANILE)*

The giant cerith is a gastropod. It dates from the Late Cretaceous period to the present. Giant ceriths are found along the bottoms of shallow, warm seas. They feed on algae. The shell of the giant cerith is often what's fossilized. It is spiraled and grows to a point. The shell can have as many as 30 spiral whorls with rows of knobs. The giant cerith drags its shell as it crawls, so one side of its shell is often flattened.

HOW TO SPOT

Size: 12 to 24 inches (30 to 61 cm) long

Identifying Features: Spiral shell

Range: Worldwide

Habitat: Warm, shallow seas

FOSSIL SIZE

Fossils come in many different shapes and sizes. Microfossils, such as bacteria and pollen, can be seen only with microscopes. Macrofossils, such as dinosaur bones and petrified trees, can be many feet long and weigh several tons.

GLASS SPONGE *(RHIZOPOTERION)*

Glass sponges in the genus *Rhizopoterion* existed in Europe during the Cretaceous period. The glass sponge was an aquatic animal. It lived on the ocean floor. It had surface pores that let water flow in and out of it. The sponge had a tall, funnel-shaped body. Glass sponge fossils are found in sedimentary rocks that were once covered by ancient seas.

HOW TO SPOT

Size: 4 inches (10 cm) tall
Identifying Features: Funnel shaped
Range: Europe
Habitat: Muddy ocean floors at depths of more than 20,000 feet (6,096 m)

GOOSE BARNACLE *(STRAMENTUM)*

Goose barnacles lived during the Cretaceous period. They were aquatic animals. Their bodies and legs were enclosed in shells. These shells had hard, overlapping plates. Goose barnacles could be fossilized if their bodies were buried in silt. The silt would then have to become a sedimentary rock.

FUN FACT

People once believed that goose barnacle fossils grew into geese, which is how they got their common name.

HOW TO SPOT

Size: 0.75 inches (1.9 cm) long

Identifying Features: Oval shaped

Range: Europe, North Africa, and North America

Habitat: Often attached to gastropods, ammonites, or bivalves on seafloors

HORN CORAL *(SEPTASTRAEA)*

Horn corals lived in the Miocene to Pleistocene epochs. They resided in warm, shallow waters near reefs. They sometimes attached to the shells of other marine animals. Horn corals had hard, star-shaped cavities. These gave the corals honeycombed appearances.

HOW TO SPOT

Size: One cavity is 0.063 inches (0.16 cm) long

Identifying Features: Large, branching colonies

Range: Atlantic coastal plains of North America and Europe

Habitat: Warm, shallow waters near reefs

PHYLLOCERATID *(PHYLLOCERAS)*

Phylloceratids were common all over the world during the Early Jurassic to Late Cretaceous periods. However, they became extinct at the same time as the dinosaurs, about 65 million years ago. A phylloceratid is a type of ammonite. Its fossil has a smooth, curved shell with dark, wavy lines. The fossils are preserved in mud that hardens into sedimentary rocks.

HOW TO SPOT

Size: 4 inches (10 cm) long
Identifying Features: Curled, smooth shell
Range: Worldwide
Habitat: Seas

FUN FACT

Phylloceratid fossils can be found in quarries, seacoasts, river shores, deserts, and canyons.

MARY ANNING

Mary Anning was born in Lyme Regis, England, in 1799. At the time, women were not encouraged to get an education. However, Anning taught herself about fossils and paleontology. She found ammonite specimens and other fossils. Anning also discovered the first complete skeleton of an ichthyosaur, an extinct aquatic reptile.

SAND DOLLAR *(ENCOPE)*

Sand dollars have been around since the Miocene epoch. They bury themselves in the sand in warm, shallow waters. These animals have rigid skeletons. They are very flat and thin with slightly domed tops. Sand dollars have flower-like patterns on their tops. The edges of these animals have slits. Living sand dollars are deep brown or purplish red. When fossilized, sand dollars can be brown or white.

HOW TO SPOT

Size: 3.5 inches (8.9 cm) long

Identifying Features: Round with flower-like patterns

Range: North and South America

Habitat: Warm, shallow waters

FUN FACT

Sand dollars got their name because sometimes their remains are silvery white and look like silver dollars.

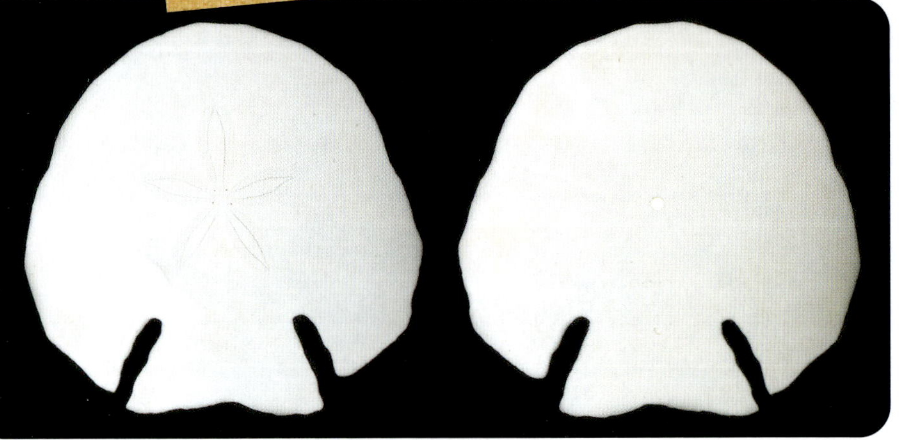

SCALLOP *(PECTEN)*

A scallop has two shells connected by a ligament. The shells have broad ribs that start at the base and spread upward. Scallops have been around since the Late Eocene epoch. They are found all over the world. These animals prefer to live in clean sands and fairly shallow waters. They often dig depressions in seabed sands and rest in them. Scallop fossils are usually just the shells. The ligament connecting the shells is rarely preserved.

HOW TO SPOT

Size: 3.1 inches (7.9 cm) long
Identifying Features: Ribbed shell
Range: Worldwide
Habitat: Clean sands and shallow waters

FUN FACT
Scallops can swim by opening and closing their hinged shells.

GETTING PRESERVED

For something to be preserved as a fossil, it needs to meet certain conditions that stop the decaying process. For instance, the organism needs to be protected from water and air. Many fossils are found in marine or freshwater sediments. In these environments, the animals were buried in oxygen-deprived clay or silt. They were able to form into fossils.

SEA LILY *(PARISANGULOCRINUS)*

Sea lilies belonging to the genus *Parisangulocrinus* lived during the Silurian to Carboniferous periods. Most were attached to seabeds by flexible stems. At the tops of the stems were cups. A series of feathery arms formed crowns on top of the cups. They filtered food from the water. Sea lilies sank to the ocean floor when they died. They were so numerous that the skeletons of their stems formed thick layers that became limestone, preserving them.

HOW TO SPOT

Size: Cup is 0.6 inches (1.5 cm) long
Identifying Features: Feathery arms
Range: Europe and North America
Habitat: Warm, shallow waters

SERPULID WORM *(GLOMERULA)*

The serpulid worm dates from the Early Jurassic period to the Paleocene epoch. The worm lived in a hard, narrow tube made of calcite. Many worms usually twisted together in tangled groups. Over many years, some of the tubes these worms made were fossilized.

HOW TO SPOT

Size: 4 inches (10 cm) long
Identifying Features: Narrow tube or a tangled mass
Range: Worldwide
Habitat: Seabeds

TRILOBITE *(OLENELLUS)*

A trilobite gets its name from the three long lobes that make up its body. It also has a head shield, a thorax with dozens of segments, and a tail shield. This creature had large eyes and a small tail. Trilobites were alive during the Early Cambrian period. They are extinct today. These animals lived in ocean environments close to seabeds.

HOW TO SPOT

Size: 2.5 inches (6.4 cm) long

Identifying Features: Small tail, large head, and many segments making up the thorax

Range: North America and Scotland

Habitat: Near seabeds

FUN FACT

Many trilobites could roll themselves into balls. Some could even lock their tails onto their head shields.

TUSK SHELL *(DENTALIUM)*

Tusk shells come from invertebrates in the scaphopod and chiton families. They've been around since the Middle Triassic period. The animals live on seafloors. They survive at different temperatures and depths. A tusk shell has between four and 20 sharp, regularly spaced ribs running along its entire length. Its smaller end is curved. The larger end has the invertebrate's head and tentacled feet, though the soft tissue is rarely fossilized.

HOW TO SPOT

Size: 2 inches (5 cm) long; 0.25 inches (0.64 cm) wide

Identifying Features: Narrow, tubular shell shaped like a tusk

Range: Worldwide

Habitat: Seafloors

FUN FACT

A scaphopod will bury itself in the sand, but it makes sure that the narrow end of its shell sticks out. From this end, the scaphopod waves its delicate tentacles in the water. This helps the animal pick up small bits of food.

ARCHAEOPTERYX *(ARCHAEOPTERYX)*

Archaeopteryx is a genus of feathered dinosaurs. They lived during the Late Jurassic period. Scientists believe these vertebrates were a transitional species between non-avian dinosaurs and birds. Fossils show that *Archaeopteryx* had wings, feathers, teeth, functioning fingers, and bony tails.

HOW TO SPOT

Size: 20 inches (51 cm) long

Identifying Features: Chicken-sized dinosaur with a long, bony tail

Range: Europe

Habitat: Near inland seashores

An artist's depiction of what *Archaeopteryx* may have looked like

ARTHRODIRE *(COCCOSTEUS)*

The arthrodire belonged to a family of primitive fish. It lived in the Middle Devonian period. An arthrodire had slicing plates instead of teeth, which wore down with use. Its head was guarded by a bony shield. A circle of bony plates protected its eyes. Its fossils have been found in sandstone.

HOW TO SPOT

Size: 14 inches (36 cm) long

Identifying Features: Broad and flattened skull, plates, and protective head shield

Range: Europe and North America

Habitat: Shallow, freshwater lakes

FUN FACT
An arthrodire could open its jaw very wide. This made it possible for the animal to eat a large variety of prey.

Head of an arthrodire

BAROSAURUS

Barosaurus was a large dinosaur that lived during the Late Jurassic period. It was a plant eater, and its long neck helped it reach treetops. *Barosaurus* likely lived near water where trees and vegetation were found. Only parts of *Barosaurus* fossils have been discovered. In fact, *Barosaurus* fossils are so rare that the skull of this dinosaur has never been found.

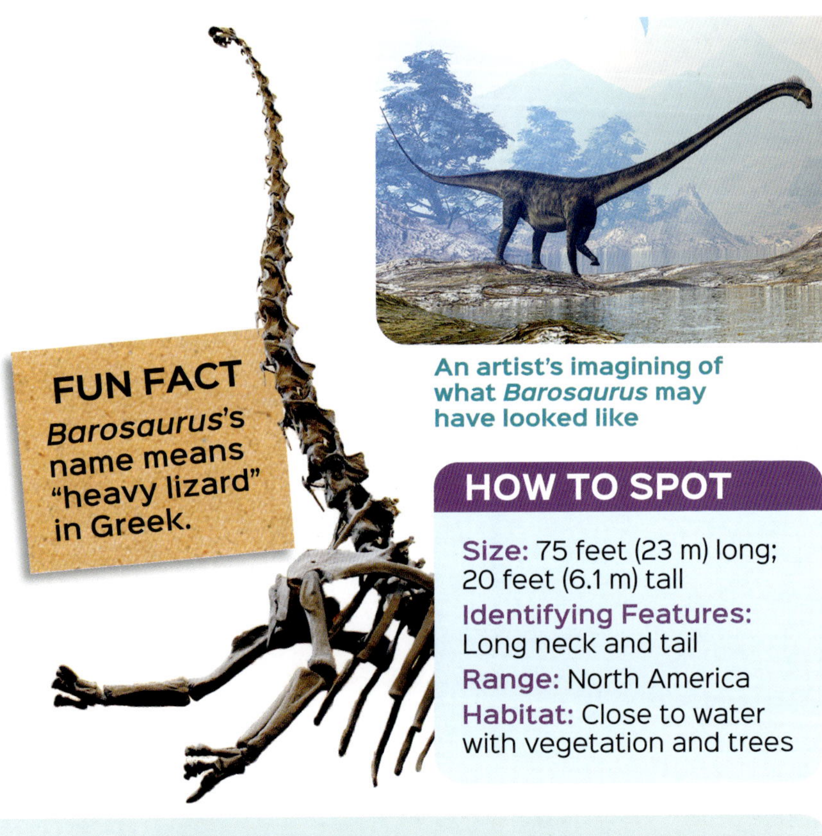

An artist's imagining of what *Barosaurus* may have looked like

FUN FACT
Barosaurus's name means "heavy lizard" in Greek.

HOW TO SPOT

Size: 75 feet (23 m) long; 20 feet (6.1 m) tall
Identifying Features: Long neck and tail
Range: North America
Habitat: Close to water with vegetation and trees

DISCOVERING *BAROSAURUS*

In the 1800s, a woman named E. R. Ellerman found the first *Barosaurus* specimen in South Dakota. She contacted a paleontologist at Yale University about the discovery, but it took years for professionals to come and excavate the skeleton. During that time, some people went to the site and took pieces of the skeleton for themselves.

DIMETRODON *(DIMETRODON)*

Dimetrodon lived during the Early Permian period. It is an extinct relative of early mammals. The most distinguishing feature of this animal is the large, sail-like structure that stood upright on its back. It also had a narrow skull and teeth of different sizes. At the front of its jaw were sharp canine teeth. These were used to rip into prey. At the back of its mouth were shearing teeth that helped *Dimetrodon* grind up bones and tough muscles.

HOW TO SPOT

Size: More than 11.5 feet (3.5 m) long
Identifying Features: Large dorsal sail and narrow skull
Range: North America
Habitat: Arid regions and wet, swampy areas

DIPLOMYSTUS *(DIPLOMYSTUS)*

Diplomystus lived from the Cretaceous period to the Eocene epoch. The fish had a bony internal skeleton. Its upturned mouth was typical in fish that fed from the water's surface. *Diplomystus* was common in many North American lakes. Its fossils have been found in the Green River Formation in Utah, Colorado, and Wyoming. This was a large lake with a muddy bottom.

HOW TO SPOT

Size: 8 inches (20 cm) long

Identifying Features: Notched tail; upturned mouth; and thin, oval scales

Range: North and South America

Habitat: Freshwater lakes

FUN FACT

Some *Diplomystus* fossils have smaller fish preserved in their mouths or intestines.

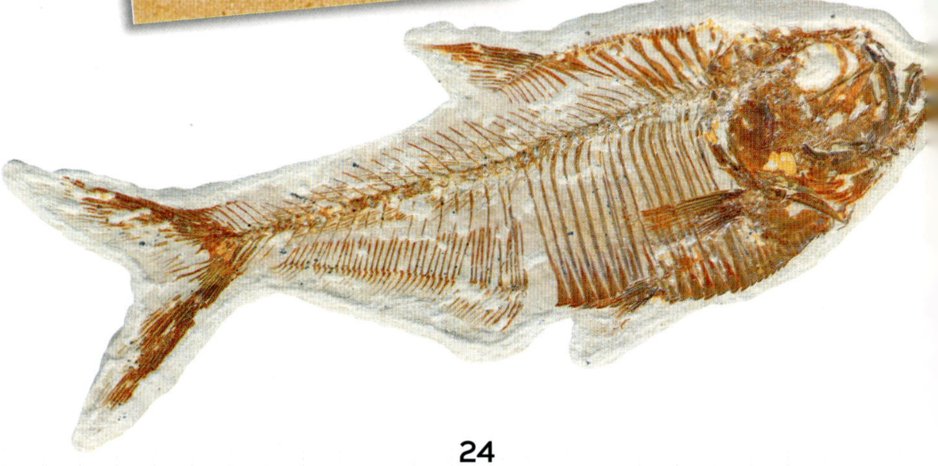

EOHIPPUS *(HYRACOTHERIUM)*

Eohippus lived during the Late Paleocene and Early Eocene epochs. This mammal is related to horses, and its feet were adapted for running. However, *Eohippus*'s body was more bent over than that of a modern horse. Its teeth were specially adapted for eating fruit and soft leaves.

HOW TO SPOT

Size: Shoulder height of 16 inches (41 cm) on average

Identifying Features: Four toes on its front feet and three toes on its back feet. Each toe had a tiny hoof.

Range: Europe and North America

Habitat: Tropical forests

FUN FACT

Many *Eohippus* fossils have been found in the Green River Formation in Utah, Colorado, and Wyoming.

ICHTHYOSAUR *(ICHTHYOSAURUS)*

The ichthyosaur was a marine reptile. It thrived during the Triassic and Jurassic periods. The animal may have swum like an eel, swinging from side to side. Its fins were like paddles. The ichthyosaur's strong eye bones indicate it could probably dive very deep in the ocean. However, the animal did not have gills, so it would have needed to surface often to breathe. Some of the best-preserved ichthyosaur fossils in the world were found in Nevada's limestone deposits.

HOW TO SPOT

Size: 6.5 feet (2 m) long on average

Identifying Features: Many teeth, a long jaw, and bony plates around its eye sockets

Range: Europe, Greenland, and North America

Habitat: Deep waters

IGUANODON *(IGUANODON)*

Iguanodon was a large, heavy, plant-eating dinosaur. It lived during the Late Jurassic and Early Cretaceous periods. *Iguanodon* primarily spent its time moving around on four legs, but it could also walk on its two hind ones. *Iguanodon* had a long tail to help it balance. Most *Iguanodon* fossils have been found in sedimentary rocks in England and Europe.

HOW TO SPOT

Size: 30 feet (9.1 m) long

Identifying Features: A long skull with jaws that end in a beak-like shape, and heavy front limbs

Range: Europe, Asia, Africa, and North America

Habitat: Forests

An artist's depiction of what *Iguanodon* may have looked like

FUN FACT

Iguanodon was first discovered in 1822 by Mary Ann Mantell. She saw some strange rocks on the side of the road. The rocks contained *Iguanodon* teeth.

MAMMOTH *(MAMMUTHUS)*

Mammoths were large mammals, weighing about 6.6 to 11 tons (6 to 10 metric tons). They lived from the Pliocene to the Early Holocene epochs. Mammoths had thick, shaggy coats. They were plant eaters who grazed on grasses, low shrubs, roots, and small plants. Mammoths often foraged for these things by digging under the snow. Mammoths lived in the cold regions of the Arctic, Siberia, and Canada. Some intact mammoth bodies have been found frozen in the Arctic permafrost.

HOW TO SPOT

Size: Shoulder height of up to 11.5 feet (3.5 m); tusks are between 5 and 9 feet (1.5 and 2.7 m) long

Identifying Features: Skeleton resembles modern elephant bones, including tusks

Range: Europe, Asia, North America, and the Arctic

Habitat: Areas with low shrubs and grasses

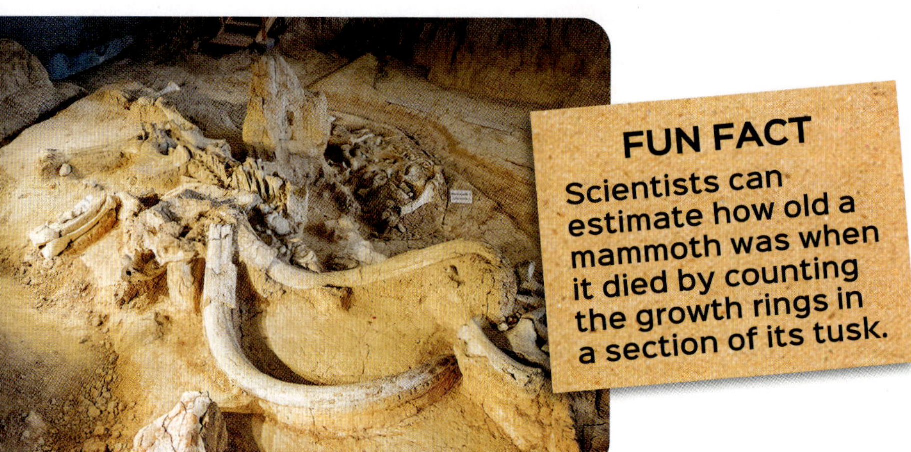

FUN FACT

Scientists can estimate how old a mammoth was when it died by counting the growth rings in a section of its tusk.

MEGALOCEPHALUS
(MEGALOCEPHALUS)

Megalocephalus was a member of the baphetids amphibian group. It lived in the Late Carboniferous period. It was a fierce predator. *Megalocephalus* evolved to have toes and to lay its eggs on land. This means the amphibian could live out of the water.

HOW TO SPOT

Size: 6.5 feet (2 m) long
Identifying Features: Crocodile-like skull and keyhole-shaped eye sockets
Range: Europe and North America
Habitat: Near swamps

Megalocephalus **head**

NEANDERTHAL
(HOMO NEANDERTHALENSIS)

Neanderthals were mammals that lived during the Late Pleistocene epoch. They are the closest extinct relative that humans have. Neanderthals had heavy eyebrow ridges. They also had smaller foreheads and chins than modern humans. Neanderthals possessed larger noses and stockier bodies too. Neanderthals lived in both temperate and cold climates. Many of their fossils have been found in caves and quarries in Europe.

HOW TO SPOT

Size: 5.1 to 5.5 feet (1.6 to 1.7 m) tall; 119 to 143 pounds (54 to 65 kg)

Identifying Features: Prominent brow ridge and a small forehead and chin

Range: Europe and central to southwestern Asia

Habitat: Wide ranging, from cold, flat, unforested grasslands to warm woodlands

FUN FACT

Neanderthals created complex tools, made jewelry, and decorated caves with art.

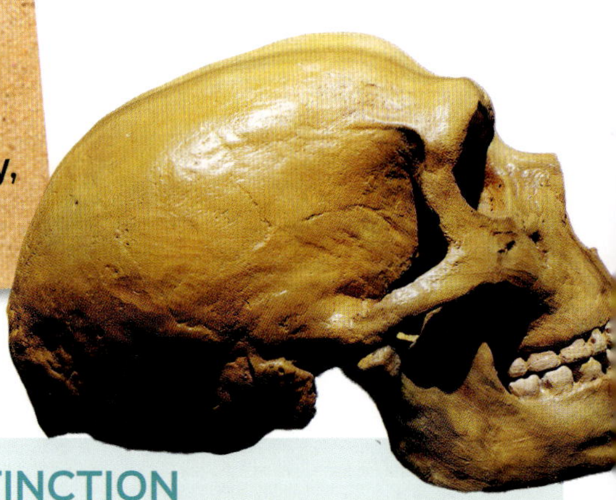

CAUSES OF EXTINCTION

Scientists aren't entirely sure why Neanderthals went extinct. Some think disease played a role. Others say the Neanderthal population was small near the end of the species' lifespan. Declining birth rates, inbreeding, and an unbalanced number of the sexes could have made the species go extinct.

SPINY SHARK *(CHEIRACANTHUS)*

The spiny shark lived during the Devonian period. It had a gaping jaw and teeth that grew in whorls. The spiny shark also had a blunt head and an upturned tail that made it a strong swimmer. It lived in freshwater lakes and rivers and swam at both mid-level and surface-level depths. Whole fossils have been found in Scotland. The fossils are often found in sandstone.

HOW TO SPOT

Size: 12 inches (30.5 cm) long

Identifying Features: One dorsal fin, three lower fins protected by spines, small scales, and an upturned tail

Range: Europe and Antarctica

Habitat: Freshwater lakes and rivers

STEREOSTERNUM *(STEREOSTERNUM)*

Stereosternum was part of a group of small, swimming reptiles that lived in the Early Permian period. This animal had fine, sharp teeth that may have been used to filter out small fish in the sea. It had webbed hands and feet and a flattened tail to help it move through the water. This animal most likely lived in shallow seawaters. Its fossils have been found in South America and South Africa.

HOW TO SPOT

Size: 12 inches (30.5 cm) long

Identifying Features: Long, needle-like teeth; an elongated head and body; short limbs; and a flattened tail

Range: South Africa and South America

Habitat: Shallow seawaters

THEROPOD TRACE FOSSIL
(THEROPOD)

Theropods were a group of dinosaurs that varied in size, from the massive *Tyrannosaurus rex* to the *Microraptor* that was the size of a crow. Trace fossils are imprints that animals left behind. They give people clues to animals' activities. Footprints are examples of trace fossils. Theropods had three-toed, bird-like tracks with claw marks and heel impressions. Fossils formed when theropods stepped in sand or mud and the sediments hardened, eventually turning into rocks and fossilizing the footprints.

HOW TO SPOT

Size: Varies depending on the species
Identifying Features: Three toes and a V-shaped outline
Range: Worldwide
Habitat: Varies but includes coastal areas, floodplains, and forests

TYRANNOSAURUS REX
(TYRANNOSAURUS)

Tyrannosaurus rex lived during the Late Cretaceous period. Its name means "king of the tyrant lizards," and it was the largest dinosaur in its genus. The *Tyrannosaurus rex* walked on its hind legs and used its tail to balance its long body. This dinosaur was a fearsome predator. It had a large head, and its jaws were filled with serrated teeth that ripped into flesh.

HOW TO SPOT

Size: 40 feet (12 m) long; 11,000 to 15,000 pounds (4,990 to 6,800 kg)

Identifying Features: Massive body with a large head and sharp teeth

Range: Western North America

Habitat: Humid, semitropical areas with open forests, rivers, and coastal swamps

FUN FACT

Tyrannosaurus rex had two big holes in its skull. Scientists think the holes held blood vessels to help the animal control its temperature.

34

WHORL-TOOTHED SHARK
(HELICOPRION)

The whorl-toothed shark lived in the Early Permian period. It is related to modern sharks and skates. When a whorl-toothed shark died, its cartilage skeleton generally dissolved, leaving only its teeth and scales to be preserved in mud and fossilized in sedimentary rock. Most fossils have been found in the southwestern United States and in Russia's Ural Mountains. The whorl-toothed shark had distinctive teeth that were coiled and created a circular whorl. The shark kept its old teeth even after growing new ones.

HOW TO SPOT

Size: 18 feet (5.5 m) long
Identifying Features: Triangular teeth that grew in a spiral
Range: Worldwide
Habitat: Seas at mid-level depths

AMBER

Amber is fossilized tree resin. It can be found as a rounded pebble or lump, or even as a stalactite where a flow of sap has hardened. Amber formed when ancient conifer trees split open or were damaged. The trees produced resins to flow into and heal the damaged bark. Amber is found worldwide, and it comes in many yellow hues with shades of brown, orange, and sometimes red. Amber that appears milky white is known as bone amber.

HOW TO SPOT

Size: Varies from small drops to fist sizes

Identifying Features: Can be either smooth or spiky in shape; sometimes has air bubbles trapped inside

Range: Worldwide

Habitat: Pine forests

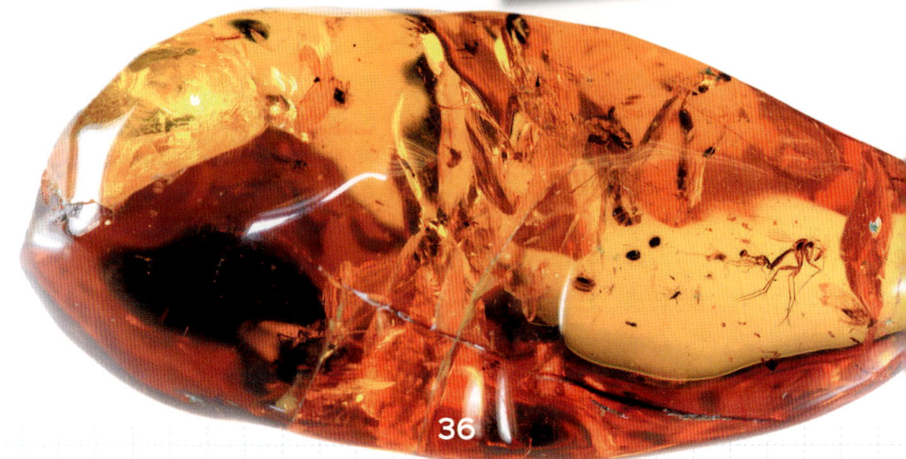

FUN FACT
Fossilized remains of insects or plants can sometimes be found inside amber.

CORDAITES *(CORDAITES)*

Cordaites is a genus of extinct plants that grew during the Late Carboniferous to Early Permian periods. The genus included both trees and shrub-like plants. The plants thrived in both wet and dry areas. Their long stems or trunks were topped by crowns of leaves. *Cordaites* fossils have impressions of leaves, seeds, and petrified wood. These fossils have been found all over the world, including in North and South America, Europe, Asia, Australia, and Africa.

HOW TO SPOT

Size: *Cordaites* grew 33 feet (10 m) tall on average

Identifying Features: Large, long leaves growing in tight spirals around stems

Range: Worldwide

Habitat: Hummocks and mangrove swamps

Illustration of what *Cordaites* may have looked like

Fossilized section of a leaf

GIANT CLUB MOSS *(LEPIDODENDRON)*

The giant club moss is part of an extinct species of trees that existed during the Carboniferous period. The giant club moss had a tall, straight trunk covered in scale-like bark. The plant had grass-like leaves and cigar-shaped cones. The giant club moss thrived in swamps. Most giant club moss fossils are either imprints of leaves or sections of bark.

HOW TO SPOT

Size: The giant club moss grew 100 feet (30 m) tall on average

Identifying Features: Leaves that look like stems of grasses; bark with diamond-shaped scales

Range: Worldwide

Habitat: Hot, humid swamps

FUN FACT
The giant club moss grew quickly, but it lived only between ten and 15 years.

GINKGO *(GINKGO)*

Ginkgo trees date from the Late Triassic to the present day. They have fan-shaped leaves and nuts with a bad smell. Ginkgo trees prefer full sun. They do well in locations near well-drained water sources. The seeds and leaves of these trees are often preserved in sedimentary rocks, such as mudstone. The oldest ginkgo fossils have been found in Russia.

FUN FACT

Ginkgo trees are known as "living fossils" because they have changed very little over millions of years.

HOW TO SPOT

Size: Ginkgo trees grow 115 feet (35 m) tall on average

Identifying Features: Fan- or wedge-shaped leaves; spherical seeds

Range: Worldwide

Habitat: Near well-drained water sources in full sun

GREEN ALGA *(MASTOPORA)*

Green algae in the *Mastopora* genus lived between the Ordovician and Silurian periods. The algae had clusters of thalli, which are bodies that don't have distinct sections, such as leaves or stems. As a result, algae fossils have spherical structures that are typically around 3 inches (8 cm) long. The fossils have honeycombed patterns. Green algae can be found in saltwater seas, especially near coral reefs. The fossils are often found in deposits of limestone and mudstone.

HOW TO SPOT

Size: 3 inches (8 cm) long

Identifying Features: Dome-shaped structure covered with a honeycomb pattern

Range: Worldwide

Habitat: Saltwater seas near coral reefs

FUN FACT
Calcium chloride crystals fall off dead algae clusters. These crystals can help build coral reefs.

HORSETAIL *(EQUISETITES)*

Horsetails belonging to the *Equisetites* genus lived from the Late Carboniferous to Late Cretaceous periods. These horsetails preferred wetland conditions, such as swamps. They had ribbed stems. These plants also had small, scale-like leaves covering their bases. Horsetail fossils are usually stems and leaves preserved in sedimentary rocks.

Equisetites tubers

FUN FACT
People can see some horsetail fossils at Petrified Forest National Park in Arizona.

HOW TO SPOT

Size: 20 inches (51 cm) tall

Identifying Features: Ribbed, stemmed plants with jointed grass-like leaves growing in whorls; underground stems and tubers; small cones

Range: Worldwide

Habitat: Wetlands

MONKEY PUZZLE TREE
(ARAUCARIA)

The monkey puzzle tree has been around since the Jurassic period. Its distinctive leaves are leathery and needle-like. The tree produces nuts and has large, spiny cones. It grows in semitropical mountain forests. Fossilized remains of this tree can include leaves, cones, bark, and nuts.

HOW TO SPOT

Size: A monkey puzzle tree grows 100 feet (30 m) tall on average

Identifying Features: Small, needle-like leaves arranged in a spiral with large, spiny cones

Range: Worldwide

Habitat: Semitropical mountain forests

PALM TREE *(PALMOXYLON)*

Palm trees belonging to the extinct genus *Palmoxylon* are similar to today's palm trees. They lived in the Paleocene through Pliocene epochs. The plants grew from single-seed leaves. *Palmoxylon* lived in semitropical forests and woodlands. Some of their trunks became petrified wood fossils.

HOW TO SPOT

Size: This tree was 65 feet (20 m) tall on average

Identifying Features: Dark, round spots on light backgrounds that lack growth rings

Range: Worldwide

Habitat: Semitropical forests and woodlands

SIGILLARIA *(SIGILLARIA)*

Sigillaria is a genus of extinct trees that lived during the Carboniferous period. These trees had tall trunks covered in thick bark. The tops of the trees sprouted leaves. These long leaves grew in spirals, but the leaves only attached near the tips of the branches. Farther down on the branches, the leaves fell off and left polygonal scars. *Sigillaria* trees grew in river floodplains. Fossilized remains of these plants include trunks, leaves, and bark.

HOW TO SPOT

Size: Up to 98 feet (30 m) tall
Identifying Features: Long, thin leaves and thick trunk
Range: South Africa
Habitat: River floodplains

TREE FERN *(PECOPTERIS)*

Tree ferns that belonged to the *Pecopteris* genus grew during the Late Carboniferous and Early Permian periods. Tree ferns thrived in swamps. They had large fronds, but most broke down before they could be fossilized. Today, people often find only small fragments of a fossilized leaf, which juts out from a single long stem.

FUN FACT

During the Carboniferous period, the landscape was dominated by plants. These plants included both massive trees that grew 100 feet (30 m) tall and small shrubs.

HOW TO SPOT

Size: Tree ferns grew 13 feet (4 m) tall on average

Identifying Features: A long stem with fossilized leaves sticking out of it

Range: Worldwide

Habitat: Swamps

ANDESITE

Andesite is often found near volcanoes and lava flows in places where tectonic plates meet. The rock forms from the lava flows after an eruption from a stratovolcano. This type of cone-shaped volcano is made from layers of hardened ash and lava. Andesite may have white, gray, or black crystals. These are formed by rapidly cooling lava.

FUN FACT

Andesite gets its name from the Andes Mountains, which lie on the western edge of South America. This rock is commonly found there.

HOW TO SPOT

Color: Brown to dark gray

Identifying Features: Glassy white, gray, or black crystals

Mineral Composition: Plagioclase, pyroxene, hornblende, biotite, and magnetite

Range: Near volcanic areas

TECTONIC PLATES

The outer layer of Earth is made up of large slabs of strong rocks called tectonic plates. These plates glide over Earth's mantle and collide with each other, causing earthquakes. Convergent boundaries are where plates collide. A subduction zone is where one plate slips beneath another. Transform boundaries are where plates slip sideways past each other.

BASALT

Basalt forms when basaltic lava cools quickly. This process often happens underwater, when lava gets pushed from Earth's mantle onto the seafloor. Cold water presses down on it from all sides. This quickly cools the lava and creates basalt. If an ocean hotspot keeps producing lava, basalt rocks may eventually reach the ocean's surface and form islands.

FUN FACT

Basalt is the most prevalent type of rock on Earth's crust. Most of the ocean floor is covered with it.

HOW TO SPOT

Color: Often black, or black with a greenish tint

Identifying Features: Fine grained

Mineral Composition: Plagioclase and pyroxene, though the rock may have small amounts of olivine, magnetite, or quartz

Range: Worldwide

INTRUSIVE AND EXTRUSIVE

Igneous rocks can be either intrusive or extrusive. Intrusive igneous rocks are created when magma cools slowly under Earth's surface. These rocks include diabase, gabbro, and granite. Extrusive rocks form when lava and ash on Earth's surface cool and solidify quickly. Andesite and basalt are examples of extrusive igneous rocks.

DACITE

Dacite is often found above subduction zones. The lava flow that occurs in these areas can form dacite. The minerals found in a particular piece of dacite will determine its color. For example, plagioclase and quartz create a white to light gray rock. Hornblende and biotite create dacite that is light gray to light brown.

HOW TO SPOT

Color: Usually light colored, such as white, light gray, or light brown

Identifying Features: Fine grained

Mineral Composition: Plagioclase is the most abundant mineral in this rock, though other minerals may include quartz, biotite, hornblende, augite, and enstatite

Range: Europe, New Zealand, South America, western North America, and elsewhere

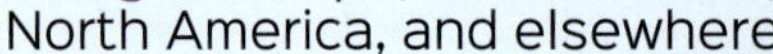

DIABASE

Diabase is often black to dark gray. It is a fine- or medium-grained rock. It forms when lava cools at a moderate rate. Diabase often has a lot of the mineral plagioclase in it. When polished, this mineral makes the rock look reflective. Because of this, some people use diabase as a stone for monuments or other architectural structures.

HOW TO SPOT

Color: Dark gray, black, or greenish black; can weather to a rusty brown

Identifying Features: Fine- or medium-grained rock with large crystals

Mineral Composition: Plagioclase makes up approximately 40 to 70 percent of diabase. Pyroxene minerals are also found in the rock, and sometimes small amounts of hornblende, olivine, magnetite, and quartz will be there too.

Range: Widespread, including in Wales, Canada, and the United States

DIORITE

Diorite is often medium to dark gray with flecks of other colors, such as light gray and white. These coarse-grained rocks are often found in formations such as sills or dikes that form above places where ocean plates are forced below continental plates. The movement of the tectonic plates releases melted magma that mixes with the granite crust and forms crystals beneath the surface, creating diorite.

FUN FACT

The Inca and Maya civilizations of South America and many ancient civilizations in the Middle East used diorite to build their structures.

HOW TO SPOT

Color: Medium to dark gray with speckles of light gray, white, dark green, or black

Identifying Features: A salt-and-pepper appearance due to the flecks of mineral grains

Mineral Composition: Plagioclase with smaller amounts of hornblende, biotite, and pyroxene

Range: In areas that have a lot of silicon-rich rocks

GABBRO

Gabbro forms when magma below Earth's surface cools very slowly. The rock is exposed when uplift pushes it to the surface. This rock can also be seen in flood basalt formations, where large amounts of basalt erupted and spread over large areas. These are found in the Columbia River area of Washington, Idaho, and Oregon.

HOW TO SPOT

Color: Speckled with dark and light colors

Identifying Features: Medium or coarse grained, often with layers of darker and paler rock; layers can be less than 1 inch (2.5 cm) or as thick as several feet, depending on how the gabbro cooled

Mineral Composition: Plagioclase, pyroxene, and rarely quartz; sometimes olivine is also present, creating a rock called olivine gabbro

Range: In thick lava flows that have basalt compositions

FUN FACT

People sometimes call gabbro "black granite." It is often used for cemetery markers, signs, and polished stone counters and floors.

GRANITE

Granite has visible grains. This rock is paler than other igneous rocks and can be pink, reddish, and white. Sometimes it is dark gray flecked with black. Granite forms deep within Earth's crust, cooling very slowly over long periods of time. It reaches the surface through uplift and is often found in mountain ranges. People often use this rock as a building stone or for block paving.

HOW TO SPOT

Color: Pink, reddish, white, or darker gray with black specks

Identifying Features: Medium or coarse grained

Mineral Composition: Quartz and feldspar with small amounts of mica, amphiboles, and other minerals

Range: Most common in mountainous regions

FUN FACT
The Mount Rushmore monument in South Dakota is carved into a mountain made of granite.

OBSIDIAN

Obsidian can be black or dark green. Sometimes it has small white patches. This is known as snowflake obsidian. The rock can also be iridescent blue, red, orange, or yellow, which is called rainbow obsidian. When the rock has swirls of brown and black, it's known as mahogany obsidian. All obsidian has a glossy appearance. This rock forms when lava solidifies very rapidly.

FUN FACT

Ancient cultures, such as the Aztecs, used obsidian tools. When obsidian fractures, it gets a very sharp edge. This made it useful for hunting.

HOW TO SPOT

Color: Black; dark green; blue, red, orange, or yellow; brown and black; some have patches of white

Identifying Features: Very smooth, glassy texture; sometimes the rocks have visible flow patterns or sharp, broken edges

Mineral Composition: Volcanic glass, quartz, and magnetite

Range: Along the edges of recent lava flows or volcanic domes, or where lava contacts water or cools while airborne

Snowflake obsidian

PUMICE

Pumice is a porous rock that is used for polishing and cleaning. Pumice forms when frothy, gas-filled lava erupts either on land or in water. When the lava cools quickly, the bubbles of gas are trapped in it, creating the small cavities found in pumice. The lava does not have time to form crystals, making pumice a form of volcanic glass. A very large volcanic eruption can create a pumice block the size of a small house.

HOW TO SPOT

Color: White or gray

Identifying Features: Many small cavities or holes

Mineral Composition: Feldspar, ferromagnesian minerals, and glassy quartz

Range: Near lava flows and volcanic eruptions

FUN FACT

Due to the pockets of gas inside it, pumice is the only rock that can float on water.

RHYOLITE

Rhyolite forms from lava that has partially cooled in Earth's subsurface before erupting. The lava usually does not flow very far. Sometimes rhyolite solidifies as a plug in the volcano as the lava cools. Rhyolite sometimes has small cavities lined with mineral crystals.

HOW TO SPOT

Color: Very light gray to whitish, light brown, or pink

Identifying Features: Fine grains and small cavities

Mineral Composition: Quartz, plagioclase, and sanidine, with small amounts of hornblende and biotite

Range: Often found near continental volcanic eruptions or eruptions that take place near the edges of continents

FUN FACT

Some gemstones, including red beryl, topaz, agate, jasper, and opal, can form in rhyolite cavities.

BRECCIA

Breccia varies in color depending on the hues of its matrix and the fragments it contains. Breccia forms where small, broken fragments of rocks or minerals accumulate and cement together. Many different rocks and minerals can combine to form breccia, and the rock often has specific names to show what it is composed of, such as sandstone breccia, limestone breccia, and chert breccia.

HOW TO SPOT

Color: Varies

Identifying Features: Made up of large fragments of other rocks, cemented together by a mineral cement or matrix mixed with very small rock particles

Mineral Composition: Varies depending on the rock fragments it includes; the matrix often contains fine particles of silt, sand, quartz, or calcite

Range: Worldwide, at the base of slopes where weathering has taken place and created small rock fragments, or in stream deposits

SEDIMENTARY ROCK FORMATION

Ice, water, and wind chip away at rocks and break them into sediments. Over time, these sediments compact and cement together, forming sedimentary rocks. Sometimes organic materials, such as bones, shells, and plants, are embedded in these rocks too. Sedimentary rocks can also form when minerals precipitate from liquids.

CHALK

Chalk is a type of limestone, and it is often light gray or white and has fine grains. Chalk forms when tiny marine organisms die and their shells sink to the ocean floor to become a sediment called ooze. Over time, ooze becomes chalk. This rock is often powdery and can be easily broken.

HOW TO SPOT

Color: Light gray or white

Identifying Features: Very porous and soft

Mineral Composition: Calcite

Range: Worldwide

FUN FACT

In the 1800s, many fossils were found in western Kansas's chalk beds. These fossils were almost totally complete. Scientists were able to study the remains of mosasaurs, plesiosaurs, and pterosaurs.

CHERT

Chert has a glossy look and smooth texture. It can be various colors, including white, brown, gray, red, green, or black. The coloring depends on how much oxygen was in the sediment when it solidified into rock. For instance, if there is a lot of oxygen, the chert may turn red. If there is not a lot of oxygen, the chert can turn black or green. This rock can be broken into smooth, sharp pieces. Because of this, throughout history many people have used chert as part of their tools or weapons.

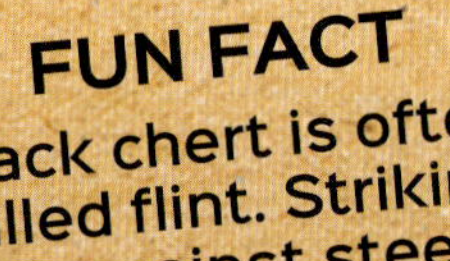

FUN FACT

Black chert is often called flint. Striking flint against steel produces sparks, and people can use these materials to start fires.

HOW TO SPOT

Color: Red, green, black, white, brown, or gray

Identifying Features: Glossy, smooth, very hard, and fractures into pieces with sharp edges

Mineral Composition: Cryptocrystalline or microcrystalline quartz

Range: In limestone and chalk formations, or where there have been deep deposits of marine sediments

COAL

Coal is composed of plant matter that once grew in or near swamps in humid, warm areas. The plant matter underwent pressure and heat. Around 10 feet (3 m) of plant matter can compress down into just 1 foot (0.3 m) of coal. People burn coal for fuel. In 2020, around 10 percent of the United States' energy consumption came from coal.

HOW TO SPOT

Color: Brown or black

Identifying Features: Shiny or dull, banded in layers, some crumbling possible

Mineral Composition: Carbonaceous plant materials, some silt and clay

Range: Worldwide, though the largest deposits are found in the United States, Russia, China, Australia, and India

CONGLOMERATE

Conglomerate is a sedimentary rock that is made up of round, often smooth fragments bigger than 0.08 inches (0.2 cm) wide. The matrix cements these fragments together. If the matrix is soft, people may crush the conglomerate to use in construction materials. If the matrix is hard, people may polish and cut the rock to use as a floor or wall decoration.

HOW TO SPOT

Color: Varies depending on the rock fragments included

Identifying Features: Chunks or grains of rock fragments that are held together by a matrix

Mineral Composition: Fragments may have particles of quartz, feldspar, or even other rocks

Range: Areas that once had flowing water or glaciers

FUN FACT

In September 2012, NASA's rover *Curiosity* was traveling across the surface of Mars. It found an area of conglomerate. Scientists believe this is evidence that water once flowed on Mars.

LIMESTONE

Limestone forms when shells, corals, algae, feces, and other organic debris accumulate. It can also form when calcium carbonate dissolves and is taken out of lakes or oceans. Limestone is a relatively soft rock. Due to that, the rock can experience weathering, and pieces of it may break off. This can create formations such as limestone cliffs and caves.

HOW TO SPOT

Color: White, tan, gray, yellow, blue, green, pink, brown, red, or black

Identifying Features: Varies, but sometimes fossils are found in limestone

Mineral Composition: Calcite

Range: Worldwide, originating in warm, shallow, and clear ocean waters

ROCK SALT

Rock salt can appear pink or red if iron oxide is present, gray if certain mineral impurities are present, and colorless or white if pure. The rock forms in large volumes of seawater or salty lake water. The salty water evaporates, leaving behind rock salt residue.

HOW TO SPOT

Color: Pink, red, gray, white, or colorless

Identifying Features: Forms a cube-like crystal shape; tastes like salt

Mineral Composition: Halite (sodium chloride) and sometimes impurities such as clay minerals, quartz, and silt

Range: In and around salt springs, salt lakes, and oceans; can also be found in underground salt domes, where heavy layers of sediment pressed down and forced salt to flow upward

FUN FACT

Salt used to be so valuable that ancient Roman soldiers were paid with it. This monthly allowance was known as *salarium*. The term evolved into the English word "salary," meaning pay.

SANDSTONE

Sandstone's color depends on its composition, but it can be white, brown, red, yellow, or green. This rock is made when particles of sand collect, compress, and get cemented together. The sand consists of minerals, rocks, or organic materials that have become smaller because of weathering. Sandstone is one of the most common sedimentary rocks.

HOW TO SPOT

Color: White, brown, red, yellow, or green

Identifying Features: Medium to fine grained; some may contain fossils

Mineral Composition: Quartz, feldspar, mica, and sometimes silt or clay, depending on the type

Range: In ancient basins where sand collected

SHALE

Shale can be black, dark gray, dark green, brown, or even red. Typically, the more organic material it has inside, the darker the shale will be. This rock is made from compacted layers of clay mud and sometimes contains fossils. Shale is often seen in large sheets. It splits into narrow layers.

HOW TO SPOT

Color: Black, dark gray, dark green, brown, or red

Identifying Features: Easily splits into long, thin-layered pieces

Mineral Composition: Quartz, mica, feldspar, clay minerals, and sometimes pyrite, calcite, and iron oxide

Range: In areas of Earth's crust where sediments accumulate

FUN FACT
Shale can be used in creating pottery, tiles, and bricks. It's also used in some cements.

TURBIDITE

Turbidites can be gray, brown, or black. These rocks form due to underwater landslides. Sediments are deposited in heavy layers on underwater slopes, and eventually sediments slide down those slopes and create sedimentary structures. Earthquakes often trigger landslides that create turbidites.

HOW TO SPOT

Color: Gray, brown, or black

Identifying Features: Layers of sediment with ripples and waves

Mineral Composition: Volcanic glass, pumice, and shells of single-celled organisms

Range: Originating in lakes and oceans, either deep in the water or near the surface if there is a steep slope present

AMPHIBOLITE

Amphibolite can be green, brown, or black. This rock forms where convergent tectonic plates trigger extreme temperatures and pressures. This process changes igneous rocks, such as basalt or gabbro, or sedimentary rocks, such as marl or graywacke, into amphibolite.

FUN FACT
Amphibolite sometimes contains garnet. This gives the rock dots of dark red coloring.

HOW TO SPOT

Color: Green, brown, or black

Identifying Features: Heavy with coarse grains; may be speckled or streaked with other minerals

Mineral Composition: Feldspar and hornblende; can also include small amounts of biotite, epidote, garnet, wollastonite, andalusite, staurolite, kyanite, sillimanite, quartz, magnetite, and calcite

Range: Worldwide

ECLOGITE

Eclogite can be light to dark gray. Sometimes it's speckled with red garnet and green pyroxene. Eclogite forms from igneous or metamorphic rocks that have high mafic mineral contents. When these rocks undergo incredibly high pressures and moderate to high temperatures, eclogite is formed.

HOW TO SPOT

Color: Light to dark gray, speckled with red and green

Identifying Features: Coarse grained, speckled with garnet and pyroxene; does not show layers

Mineral Composition: Pyroxene and garnet; can also contain disthene, quartz, and actinolite

Range: Areas near current or ancient subduction zones

TYPES OF METAMORPHISM

Metamorphic rocks can form in three ways: through regional, contact, or dynamic metamorphism. Regional metamorphism happens over a large area and through processes such as mountain formation. Contact metamorphism happens when magma makes contact with an existing rock. In dynamic metamorphism, strong forces of heat and pressure cause the rocks to bend or fold, or to get crushed, flattened, or sheared.

GNEISS

Gneiss has parallel but irregular banding on its surface. The bands are often a result of different amounts of minerals in those sections or various mineral grain sizes in the rock. Gneiss forms at plate boundaries, where heat enlarges the mineral grains. Other rocks can transform into gneiss. For instance, metamorphism changes shale into slate, then the slate can turn into phyllite, then schist, and then finally gneiss.

HOW TO SPOT

Color: Light to dark gray, brown, or lighter colors; the rock is streaked with additional colors

Identifying Features: Medium to coarse grained, light and dark areas that can be streaked or folded, and many thin layers

Mineral Composition: Feldspar, quartz, muscovite, and biotite, with smaller amounts of garnet, cordierite, sillimanite, and hornblende

Range: Lower parts of Earth's crust

MARBLE

Marble forms when limestone is exposed to high temperatures and pressures. Marble is white in its pure form. When it has other minerals inside it, the rock's color can turn to pink, gray, brown, green, yellow, blue, or black. It can also have streaks or patches of various colors. Marble has a sparkling, almost sugary appearance. This rock has many uses, such as building foundations, sculptures, and monuments.

HOW TO SPOT

Color: White, pink, gray, brown, green, yellow, blue, black, or a combination of colors, depending on the rock's minerals

Identifying Features: Medium grained and gritty

Mineral Composition: Calcite, clay minerals, mica, quartz, pyrite, iron oxide, and graphite

Range: Worldwide at convergent plate boundaries with high temperatures and pressures

FUN FACT

Sometimes colored veins appear in marble. This happens when Earth's movement cuts open the rock, creating fissures. These openings are then filled with minerals that bring more color to the rock and create a veiny appearance.

A FAMOUS MARBLE MONUMENT

The Washington Monument in Washington, DC, is made from marble. It took more than 30 years to finish the monument, and the marble came from three different places. Each quarry produced a slightly different color, so there are three shades of white in the monument.

MIGMATITE

Migmatite typically forms when lava heats up an existing metamorphic rock and melts it. The liquid rock forms a light color. The minerals within the rock stay solid and are often dark. When the new rock eventually cools, it appears dark with pale streaks.

HOW TO SPOT

Color: Dark with pale streaks

Identifying Features: Coarse with a grainy texture

Mineral Composition: Amphibole, pyroxene, and biotite mica in darker sections; feldspar, quartz, and mica in paler areas

Range: Usually found in areas where there is strong tectonic plate activity and sections of crust have been affected by high temperatures and pressures

QUARTZITE

Quartzite is usually white to gray, but minerals can color the rock red, pink, yellow, green, blue, and orange. This rock has a sandpapery feel, but people can polish the rock into a glossy shine. Quartzite forms when sandstone or chert, which are high in quartz, are exposed to extreme heat and pressure.

HOW TO SPOT

Color: White, gray, red, pink, yellow, green, blue, and orange

Identifying Features: Extremely hard material, sugary appearance, glassy shine, breaks into flat pieces

Mineral Composition: Quartz and sometimes mica

Range: Found in many mountain ranges around the world, including the Baraboo Range in Wisconsin, the Wasatch Range in Utah, the La Cloche Mountains in Canada, and Monte Binga in Mozambique

FUN FACT
Quartzite is so hard that even a metal blade can't scratch it.

SCHIST

Schist is created when compression, heat, and chemical activity turn shale into slate, then into phyllite, and finally into schist. Schist's thin layers can be split apart. This rock is grouped by what minerals are inside it. For instance, talc schist holds a lot of the mineral talc. Mica schist contains muscovite mica.

HOW TO SPOT

Color: Dark gray, green, brown, tan, or black

Identifying Features: Large grains of minerals that can be easily seen

Mineral Composition: Muscovite, chlorite, sericite, talc, graphite, and biotite

Range: Near convergent plate boundaries

SERPENTINITE

Serpentinite typically has a veiny appearance. This rock forms as a result of serpentinization. This process converts certain minerals into other minerals by pushing hot water through tiny pores and fractures in the rock. This dissolves some of the silica inside it. The silica water causes a chemical reaction that creates serpentine minerals, which make up the majority of this rock.

HOW TO SPOT

Color: Gray green, yellow green, dark green, or brown
Identifying Features: Coarse grained, flaky, and dense
Mineral Composition: Serpentine minerals
Range: Worldwide; mined in California, Arizona, New Jersey, and New York

FUN FACT
Serpentinite has a slippery feel, like snakeskin.

SKARN

Skarn can have pale or dark coloring with patches of gray, black, brown, and green. This rock is not defined by the types of minerals it has. Instead, it is defined by the process that altered it: metasomatism. This process occurs when magma heats fluids, such as water, which then interact directly with rocks such as limestones or dolostones. This morphs the original rock's structure. The resulting skarn is a coarse-grained, hard rock.

HOW TO SPOT

Color: Varies from pale to dark with additional patches of color

Identifying Features: Coarse grained and hard

Mineral Composition: Often includes calcium, iron, and magnesium

Range: Typically around the edges of magma fields

SLATE

Slate is a fine-grained rock that easily breaks into thin layers. The rock's color is determined by what mineral is in it. For instance, iron oxide produces purple or red slate. Green slate is caused by chlorite. Slate is formed from sedimentary rocks, such as shale or mudstone, that have been changed by pressure and heat.

HOW TO SPOT

Color: Black, gray, blue, purple, green, or red

Identifying Features: Smooth to the touch and breaks into sheets

Mineral Composition: Clay minerals, small amounts of quartz, mica, calcite, and feldspar; may also contain fossils

Range: Found as layers between sedimentary rocks, usually in saltwater deposits, but sometimes where lakes existed during previous ice ages

ANORTHITE

The mineral anorthite has glassy, brittle, white or gray crystals. The crystals can also be green, yellow, or a range of pink to red. Anorthite is often found in igneous and metamorphic rocks. People use this mineral to manufacture ceramics and glass.

HOW TO SPOT

Color: White, gray, green, yellow, pink, or red

Streak Color: White

Hardness: 6 to 6.5

Crystal System: Triclinic

Luster: Vitreous

Range: Major deposits are found in India, Sweden, Japan, Italy, and New Jersey in the United States

CRYSTAL SYSTEMS

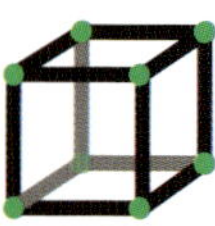

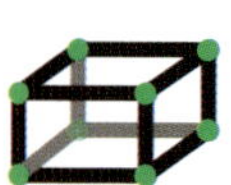

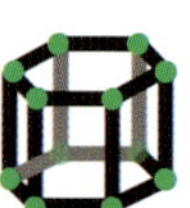

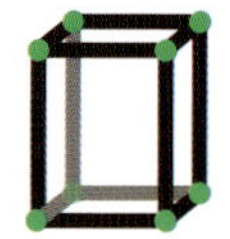

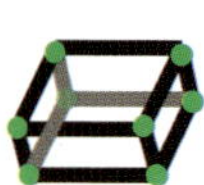

Minerals are classified by what crystal system their shapes belong to. The shape is determined by the symmetry of a mineral's crystals.

WHAT IS LUSTER?

Luster refers to how reflective a mineral's surface is. A vitreous luster looks like regular window glass. Metallic looks like polished metal. Silky may look similar to the way light shimmers on silk. A pitchy luster looks tar-like. A greasy luster looks like grease stains on paper. Adamantine appears like cut diamonds or lead crystal glass. A pearly luster looks like the inside of a shell.

ARSENIC

Arsenic looks like a mass of blackish-gray lumps. It has a metallic sheen when freshly mined, but after a few hours it turns dark and dull. Arsenic is found in Earth's crust. It is mostly mined in China and Morocco.

HOW TO SPOT

Color: Blackish gray
Streak Color: Black
Hardness: 3 to 4
Crystal System: Trigonal
Luster: Metallic to dull
Range: Found in small quantities in rock, soil, water, and air

MINERAL HARDNESS

Testing the hardness of a mineral can help identify it. The Mohs Hardness Scale measures a mineral's hardness based on its resistance to being scratched. The scale ranges from one to ten, with one being soft and ten being hard. For instance, talc is a one on the scale. It can be scratched with a fingernail. A diamond is a ten. Not many things can scratch a diamond.

BARITE

Barite can look like fan-shaped masses of crystals, or it can form as a series of rosette shapes. Some of its colors might be luminescent. Barite is often found in veins of ore, in sedimentary or igneous rocks, and in clay or marine deposits. Barite is mined in many countries, including India, China, Morocco, Iran, and the United States. The mineral can be used in the creation of cements, paints, and other materials.

FUN FACT

Barite made from sand is brown. It may have crystals that resemble flowers. These are known as barite desert roses.

HOW TO SPOT

Color: White, gray, orange, red, pink, purple, brown, blue, green, black, or colorless

Streak Color: White

Hardness: 3 to 3.5

Crystal System: Orthorhombic

Luster: Vitreous, pearly

Range: Worldwide, in sedimentary rock layers and ore veins

STREAK COLOR

Streak colors can help classify minerals. They are found by drawing lines with the minerals, usually by scraping the minerals on rough surfaces. The line colors are characteristic of certain types of minerals. Some minerals come in a variety of colors. But the streak color for a certain mineral will always be the same. For example, barite can be many different colors. But its streak color will always be white.

CALCITE

Calcite is a common mineral that can be white or colorless when pure, or almost any other color when impure. Calcite is soft and can be easily scratched by a knife. Most calcite is found in limestone. When limestone undergoes metamorphism, the calcite often recrystallizes and turns the rock into a calcite marble. Calcite and the rocks it is found in can have various uses. For instance, limestone helps make cement. Marble is used for carvings and statues.

HOW TO SPOT

Color: White, colorless, red, yellow, pink, blue, green, black, brown, or lavender

Streak Color: White

Hardness: 3

Crystal System: Trigonal

Luster: Vitreous

Range: Many countries in the world, including Mexico, the United States, India, and Germany

CALCITE IN NATURE

One type of calcite forms from calcium-rich waters inside caverns or on limestone cliffs, creating stalagmites, stalactites, and strange globular growths. These growths constantly accumulate, creating layers. They often trap organic matter such as leaves, twigs, and mosses. These things make the calcite impure.

CARNALLITE

Carnallite dissolves in cold water. It has a bitter, salty taste. If carnallite is placed in a flame, it melts easily and makes the flame purple. Carnallite can be found in the upper sections of marine salt deposits. This mineral serves as a source of potassium used in fertilizers.

HOW TO SPOT

Color: Blue, yellow, red, white, or colorless
Streak Color: White
Hardness: 2.5
Crystal System: Orthorhombic
Luster: Greasy, and transparent to translucent
Range: Northern Germany, Spain, Tunisia, and the southwestern United States

CHROMITE

Chromite is brownish black to greenish black. It is usually found as grains or crystals embedded in rocks, much like chocolate chips in cookies. Chromite has chromium in it. People extract this element and use it to create steel.

FUN FACT

Many gemstone colors occur because they contain small amounts of chromium. Red rubies, pink sapphires, and green emeralds get their colors from this element.

HOW TO SPOT

Color: Brownish black to greenish black

Streak Color: Dark brown

Hardness: 5.5

Crystal System: Cubic

Luster: Metallic to greasy

Range: Russia, India, Kazakhstan, the Philippines, New Caledonia, Kosovo, Zimbabwe, Turkey, Brazil, and Cuba

CINNABAR

Cinnabar is known for its rich red color. It is often found as a crystal on a rock's surface. Cinnabar can be found around volcanic vents and hot springs, and as mineral veins in locations with volcanic activity.

HOW TO SPOT

Color: Bright red to brownish red; sometimes gray

Streak Color: Red

Hardness: 2 to 2.5

Crystal System: Trigonal

Luster: Either adamantine or a flat matte without a glossy finish

Range: Worldwide

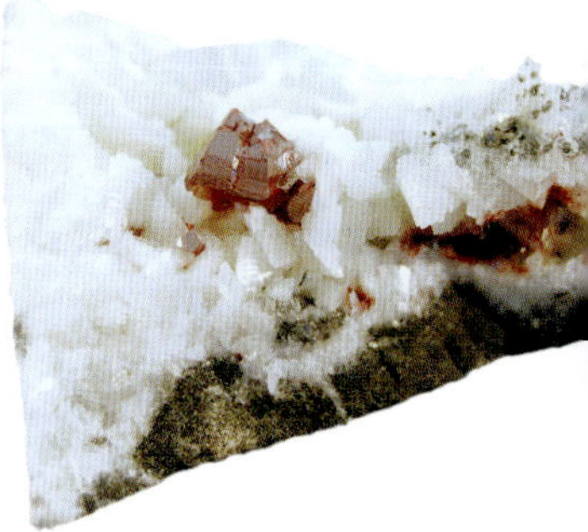

FUN FACT

Cinnabar is a mineral ore of mercury. That means cinnabar is extremely toxic. It was once used as a red pigment for paint, but it has now been replaced with safer pigments.

COPPER

Copper has a reddish, metallic sheen. It is only found in small quantities throughout the world. Copper is found in basaltic volcanic rocks or as a compound with other minerals. Copper has been used by humans for thousands of years. Around 5500 BCE, people began using copper to make tools. Today, copper can be used in wiring, plumbing, machines, car parts, and more.

Color: Reddish
Streak Color: Copper red
Hardness: 2.5 to 3
Crystal System: Cubic
Luster: Metallic
Range: Large copper ore mines exist in the United States, Canada, Bolivia, Mexico, Chile, Australia, Botswana, and Uganda

NATIVE ELEMENTS

Native elements are minerals made up of chemical elements that exist alone. They are not combined with other chemical elements to form compounds. Examples of native elements include copper, gold, antimony, arsenic, sulfur, and carbon.

CROCOITE

Crocoite is a bright, orangish-red mineral. It forms where deposits containing lead and chromium have been weathered and oxidized. Crocoite is rare because lead and chromium normally do not exist together. Crocoite melts when exposed to a flame, and it dissolves only in a strong acid. This mineral has a vitreous to adamantine luster that grows dull when exposed to sunlight.

FUN FACT

Due to crocoite's colorful crystals, this mineral is popular with collectors. Crocoite was also once used as a paint pigment.

HOW TO SPOT

Color: Orange red
Streak Color: Yellow orange
Hardness: 2.5 to 3
Crystal System: Monoclinic
Luster: Vitreous to adamantine
Range: Tasmania, Brazil, southwestern United States, and Russia

DOLOMITE

The term *dolomite* can describe both the mineral in its pure form and a type of limestone that is primarily made up of dolomite. The crystals in this mineral can be white, colorless, blue, dark to light gray, or tan. Dolomite is often found in rocks that were formed from calcium carbonate mud that was then altered by water rich in magnesium. Dolomite is often used to make cement.

HOW TO SPOT

Color: White, colorless, blue, dark to light gray, or tan
Streak Color: White
Hardness: 3.5 to 4
Crystal System: Trigonal
Luster: Vitreous or pearly

Range: The most famous quarries are located in the midwestern United States; Ontario, Canada; Switzerland; Pamplona, Spain; and Mexico

ENARGITE

The crystals in enargite are metallic gray and heavy. Sometimes the crystals are coated with thin layers of pyrite, giving them more of a yellow color. Enargite crystals are sometimes clearly arranged in long, thin, parallel streaks. Enargite is found in veins of copper ore that are rich in arsenic.

FUN FACT

Enargite is a sulfosalt, which is a type of mineral that has both sulfur and metal.

HOW TO SPOT

Color: Grayish black to black

Streak Color: Black to dark gray

Hardness: 3.5

Crystal System: Orthorhombic

Luster: Metallic

Range: Deposits are found in Montana in the United States, and in Italy, Chile, the Balkans, and Peru

FLUORITE

Fluorite is popular with collectors because of its beautiful, varied colors. This mineral is found in hydrothermal veins of heated water in Earth's crust, such as hot springs, and especially in those containing lead and zinc. Fluorite is used in steel manufacturing.

Color: Purple, golden yellow, green, colorless, blue, pink, champagne, or brown
Streak Color: White
Hardness: 4
Crystal System: Cubic
Luster: Vitreous
Range: Worldwide

FUN FACT

Fluorite glows under ultraviolet light. This mineral's name is the origin of the word *fluorescent*.

GARNET

Garnet is a group of minerals. Most form at plate boundaries where shale is metamorphosed by heat and pressure. Garnets begin as tiny grains that slowly grow over time and displace or replace the rock materials around them. Garnets are usually red, but they can be orange, green, yellow, purple, black, or brown. Blue garnets are extremely rare. Garnets are used as gemstones.

HOW TO SPOT

Color: Typically red
Streak Color: Colorless
Hardness: 6.5 to 7.5
Crystal System: Cubic
Luster: Vitreous
Range: Mined around the world, including in Australia, the United States, India, China, and more

GEMSTONES

Gemstones are minerals that are used in jewelry. Gemstones with beautiful colors are polished so that they shine and sparkle. This is especially important because some minerals in their natural states, such as diamonds, are colorless and uninteresting.

GOLD

Gold is one of the most well-known minerals. In its natural mineral form, gold almost always contains traces of silver. For instance, a gold nugget is usually 70 to 95 percent gold and the remainder is mostly silver. It may also have traces of copper and iron.

HOW TO SPOT

Color: Golden yellow, but has a lighter color when it contains silver

Streak Color: Yellow

Hardness: 2.5 to 3

Crystal System: Cubic

Luster: Metallic

Range: Mined in South Africa, Russia, Australia, Canada, and Nevada and Alaska in the United States

FUN FACT

Gold is a precious metal. In 2019, people mined about 3,892 tons (3,531 metric tons) of gold. People have used this mineral for thousands of years to create decorative objects and jewelry.

GYPSUM

Gypsum is best known for its use in making plaster. This mineral forms in deposits of evaporated water, usually where marine seas or inland lakes have dried out. It can also occur near hot springs. Gypsum crystals with sand trapped inside become brown, gray, or opaque, and the crystals may form rosettes in a desert rose flower shape.

FUN FACT

The largest gypsum crystal ever found was in Chile. It was more than 10 feet (3 m) long and 1.5 feet (0.46 m) wide.

HOW TO SPOT

Color: Colorless, white, gray, yellow, red, or brown

Streak Color: White

Hardness: 2

Crystal System: Monoclinic

Luster: Pearly

Range: Deposits located in Spain, Thailand, the United States, Turkey, and Russia

HALITE

Halite is rock salt that occurs naturally. It forms in places where salt water has evaporated, such as marine lagoons or inland salt lakes. Halite can also occur near volcanic vents. It forms when volcanic solids become gases in a process called sublimation. Halite is found on every continent. Sometimes halite beds are only about 9 to 10 feet (2.7 to 3 m) thick. Other times they are more than 1,000 feet (305 m) thick.

HOW TO SPOT

Color: Colorless, white, red, orange, yellow, purple, or blue

Streak Color: White

Hardness: 2

Crystal System: Cubic

Luster: Vitreous

Range: Large deposits are found in Russia, France, India, Ontario, and the United States

FUN FACT

In some underground halite deposits, the mineral is pushed upward by either tectonic or gravitational forces. It pops out through soft ground and forms an arched structure known as a salt dome.

HEMATITE

Hematite is found in sedimentary, metamorphic, and igneous rocks. It is the most valuable ore in iron. Hematite sometimes has enough magnetite in it to attract a common magnet. Hematite can be black or red. Some samples have steel-gray crystals with a metallic luster. Others are soft with fine grains.

FUN FACT

Hematite is one of the most common minerals found on Earth's surface and in the planet's crust.

HOW TO SPOT

Color: Black, red, or steel-gray crystals

Streak Color: Red or reddish brown

Hardness: 6.5

Crystal System: Trigonal

Luster: Metallic to dull

Range: Most often mined in China, Australia, Brazil, India, Russia, Ukraine, South Africa, Canada, Venezuela, and the United States

LAZULITE

Lazulite is popular for its range of blue colors. This mineral forms in many different geological environments, especially in veins of quartz, igneous rocks, and quartzites. It is often seen as either grains or glassy crystals. Lazulite embedded in white quartz is often cut into slabs and polished for collectors. When heated, lazulite breaks into small pieces but does not melt.

FUN FACT

Lazulite comes from the German word *lazurstein*, which means "blue stone."

HOW TO SPOT

Color: Deep azure blue, pale blue, or bluish green

Streak Color: White

Hardness: 5 to 6

Crystal System: Monoclinic

Luster: Vitreous to dull, or translucent to opaque; can be transparent in rare cases

Range: Austria, Sweden, California, and Brazil

MAGNETITE

Magnetite is the only mineral that is naturally magnetic. It can sometimes be found with small iron filings stuck to its surface. Magnetite frequently forms in rocks that come from magma and in mineral veins that contain large amounts of sulphates. Magnetite develops a reddish-brown rust when it gets wet.

HOW TO SPOT

Color: Black
Streak Color: Black
Hardness: 6 to 6.5
Crystal System: Cubic
Luster: Dull metallic
Range: Various places around the world, such as in Hong Kong, California, and the west coast of New Zealand's North Island

FUN FACT

The first magnetic compasses were made by hanging magnetite from strings. They were used in China as early as 300 BCE. When freely hanging from strings, small pieces of magnetite will align themselves with Earth's magnetic field.

NITRATINE

Nitratine is found in arid environments where it hardly ever rains. This mineral is efflorescent, meaning it loses water from its crystal structure and develops a white, powdery surface. Nitratine is used in the manufacturing of fertilizer, and it has also been used to create gunpowder.

HOW TO SPOT

Color: Colorless, white, light yellow, light gray, or light brown
Streak Color: White
Hardness: 1.5 to 2
Crystal System: Hexagonal
Luster: Vitreous
Range: Arid environments

OLIVINE

Olivine is a name for a group of minerals. One mineral in this group is forsterite. It is also known as white olivine. It has a lot of magnesium. Another mineral in this group is fayalite. It is rich in iron. The gem variety of olivine is called peridot. Olivine minerals are mostly found at Earth's surface in dark colored igneous rocks.

FUN FACT

Olivine has been identified on the Moon and Mars. It's also seen in meteorites and in a comet called Wild 2.

HOW TO SPOT

Color: Green, greenish yellow, yellow, yellowish brown, brown, white, or colorless

Streak Color: Colorless

Hardness: 6.5 to 7

Crystal System: Orthorhombic

Luster: Vitreous and slightly greasy

Range: Myanmar, Pakistan, Russia, Mexico, Brazil, Australia, Germany, Norway, Sweden, Ethiopia, China, and the United States

PYRITE

Pyrite is extremely common. It can form in both high and low temperatures and is found in igneous, metamorphic, and sedimentary rocks all over the world. Its name comes from the Greek word for fire, *pyr*. That's because pyrite gives off sparks when struck with something made of metal.

Pyrite can be confused with gold. That's because, to the untrained eye, the two seem similar in color and shape. This has led to pyrite's nickname, "fool's gold."

HOW TO SPOT

Color: Brassy yellow
Streak Color: Greenish to brownish black
Hardness: 6 to 6.5
Crystal System: Cubic
Luster: Metallic
Range: Italy, Spain, Kazakhstan, Peru, and the United States

QUARTZ

Quartz is a common mineral that forms in igneous, sedimentary, and metamorphic rocks. It is very resistant to weathering. That makes it the dominant mineral of mountaintops and the primary part of beach, river, and desert sands. Quartz can be a wide variety of colors. This mineral is used for many things, including the creation of glass, fire bricks, rubber, and paint.

HOW TO SPOT

Color: Colorless, white, gray, yellow, green, purple, pink, red, brown, or black

Streak Color: Colorless

Hardness: 7

Crystal System: Trigonal

Luster: Vitreous to greasy

Range: Worldwide, especially the Alps, Brazil, Madagascar, Japan, and the United States

FUN FACT

Well-shaped quartz crystals in the United States have been found in Hot Springs, Arkansas, and Little Falls and Ellenville, New York.

SCHEELITE

Scheelite is brown, yellow, white, or green. This mineral is found in hydrothermal, or heated, water veins and coarse-grained igneous rocks. It is also found in rocks altered by contact metamorphism. Under ultraviolet light, scheelite gives off white or bluish-white fluorescence.

HOW TO SPOT

Color: Brown, yellow, white, or green

Streak Color: White

Hardness: 4.5 to 5

Crystal System: Tetragonal

Luster: Greasy

Range: England, Bolivia, New Zealand, New South Wales, Switzerland, France, Siberia, and the United States

SILVER

Silver is a well-known mineral that is often used to make jewelry. Silver can be found in a pure state, but it is usually mixed with small amounts of gold, arsenic, and antimony. Silver is found in volcanic basalt rocks and in water veins with hot or moderate temperatures. It may also form by the breakdown of sulfur from lead or zinc deposits.

FUN FACT

Silver has many unique physical properties that give it a special status. For instance, it is a good conductor of electricity. It is also easy to either hammer silver out or stretch it into a thin wire.

HOW TO SPOT

Color: Whitish silver; tarnishes when exposed to air

Streak Color: Silvery white

Hardness: 2.5 to 3

Crystal System: Cubic

Luster: Metallic, opaque

Range: Mined in many different countries, such as the United States, Canada, Mexico, Peru, and Bolivia

SPERRYLITE

Sperrylite is often found in rocks that have been changed through contact metamorphism. Since sperrylite is very resistant to weathering, it is also found in the sand and gravel of rivers. This mineral is prized by collectors. As an ore of platinum, sperrylite is valuable as a metal ore mineral.

FUN FACT

Sperrylite is named after Francis Louis Sperry. He was a chemist who discovered this mineral in 1889.

HOW TO SPOT

Color: Gray
Streak Color: Black to dark gray
Hardness: 6 to 7
Crystal System: Cubic
Luster: Metallic
Range: Canada, Russia, South Africa, and North Carolina in the United States

SYLVANITE

Sylvanite has both gold and silver in its chemical formula. It is valued by collectors because it is rare and because it contains gold. Sylvanite forms in hydrothermal veins. It often forms with gold, quartz, fluorite, pyrite, and other sulphates. Sylvanite is often a silvery white color but can also be yellow.

HOW TO SPOT

Color: Silvery white, gray; sometimes yellowish

Streak Color: Black to dark gray

Hardness: 1.5 to 2

Crystal System: Monoclinic

Luster: Metallic

Range: Hungary, Australia, Canada, and the western United States

TOPAZ

Topaz is a mineral gemstone that can be used in jewelry. Most topaz grows as crystals within igneous rocks. Topaz in its pure form is colorless. In other cases, the mineral can be different shades of brown, blue, or yellow. In rare cases, the mineral can be red. However, the colors can change over time. For instance, brown topaz may get bleached by sunlight.

HOW TO SPOT

Color: Colorless, brown, blue, yellow, pink, or red
Streak Color: Colorless
Hardness: 8
Crystal System: Orthorhombic
Luster: Vitreous, transparent to translucent
Range: Brazil, the United States, Madagascar, Burma, Namibia, Zimbabwe, Mexico, Sri Lanka, Pakistan, Russia, and China

TORBERNITE

Torbernite forms in coarse granite or in other igneous rocks. It may also appear as a secondary mineral when the highly radioactive mineral uraninite is formed. Torbernite itself is radioactive and gives off small amounts of toxic radon gas. It is occasionally found coating the walls of crevices in rocks.

HOW TO SPOT

Color: Various shades of green
Streak Color: Pale green
Hardness: 2 to 2.5
Crystal System: Tetragonal
Luster: Sub-adamantine, vitreous, waxy, pearly
Range: England, Germany, Czech Republic, and many other places where uraninite minerals exist

FUN FACT

Torbernite is radioactive because it contains uranium. For this reason, it has to be handled carefully. Torbernite should not be kept where people live. Always wash your hands after touching this mineral. It should be stored in containers with X-ray shielding.

TURQUOISE

Turquoise is a popular mineral used in jewelry. It forms in arid climates in altered and weathered volcanic rocks. Its color can vary from greenish to blue. Sky-blue turquoise is a popular gemstone color. Some turquoise has part of its host rock in it. This looks like black patches or spider webbing. Turquoise has been prized by people for centuries. For instance, the ancient Egyptians used it to make beads and amulets.

HOW TO SPOT

Color: Greenish to blue
Streak Color: Greenish to bluish white
Hardness: 6
Crystal System: Triclinic
Luster: Waxy to dull
Range: Most come from the southwestern United States, China, Chile, Egypt, Iran, and Mexico

FUN FACT

Turquoise has been used as an ornament by Native American cultures since 200 BCE. Those making turquoise ornaments today include the Navajo, Hopi, and Zuni peoples. The ornaments are used for ceremonies, art, jewelry, and more.

URANINITE

Uraninite is often black, brown, or gray. However, it can also turn yellow, orange red, or greenish yellow. Uraninite can occur in granite. It is also found in sedimentary rocks. Uranium is the major element in uraninite. Uranium is a chemical element known for being radioactive.

FUN FACT

Uraninite is an important radioactive mineral, but it was once thought to be worthless. When its uranium content was discovered, it became valuable. Scientist Marie Curie studied radioactivity by looking at samples of uraninite.

HOW TO SPOT

Color: Black, brown, gray, yellow, orange red, or greenish yellow

Streak Color: Black, brownish black, gray, or greenish

Hardness: 5 to 6

Crystal System: Cubic

Luster: Submetallic or greasy

Range: Deposits have been found in the United States, Canada, Australia, Austria, the Czech Republic, England, Germany, Hungary, Namibia, Norway, Rwanda, and South Africa

VANADINITE

Vanadinite usually forms where lead minerals are oxidized, or chemically combined with oxygen. This often happens in areas with arid climates. Vanadinite is often a red, orange, or brown color. Many people like vanadinite for its bright colors and large crystals.

HOW TO SPOT

Color: Red, orange, or brown

Streak Color: Yellowish brown to pale yellow

Hardness: 3

Crystal System: Hexagonal

Luster: Greasy to adamantine

Range: Morocco, Namibia, Argentina, Australia, and the United States

GLOSSARY

crystal
A piece of a solid material that has molecules fitting together in a repeating pattern.

dorsal
Located near or on the back, especially of an animal.

genus
A group of related animals or plants that is narrower than a family but broader than a species.

hummocks
Rounded mounds of earth.

invertebrate
An animal that does not have a backbone.

luminescent
Emitting light that is not caused by heat.

mafic
A group of minerals that are rich in iron and magnesium.

magma
Melted rock that comes from deep inside Earth's crust and is called lava when it erupts onto the surface.

matrix
Substances such as silt and clay that hold fragments together in sedimentary rocks.

petrified
Has become hard like stone over a long period of time.

quarry
A large, deep pit where stones or other materials are extracted.

vertebrate
An animal with a backbone.

weathering
The process by which rocks or other materials are worn down by things such as water, wind, or climate.

whorl
A pattern of spirals or concentric circles.

FURTHER READINGS

Eboch, Chris. *Rocks and Minerals: Get the Dirt on Geology*. Nomad Press, 2020.

Swanson, Jennifer. *Rock, Fossil, and Shell Hunting*. Odd Dot, 2021.

Wang, Yinan. *The 50 State Fossils: A Guidebook for Aspiring Paleontologists*. Schiffer, 2018.

ONLINE RESOURCES

To learn more about fossils, rocks, and minerals, please visit **abdobooklinks.com** or scan this QR code. These links are routinely monitored and updated to provide the most current information available.

PHOTO CREDITS

Cover Photos: iStockphoto, front (conglomerate), front (amber), front (mahogany obsidian), front (calcite), back (rock salt); Minakryn Ruslan/iStockphoto, front (chert), back (fluorite); Julia Reschke/Shutterstock Images, front (gold); Albert Russ/Shutterstock Images, front (barite); Shutterstock Images, front (fluorite), front (serpentinite), back (Ichthyosaur); Sebastian Janicki/Shutterstock Images, front (quartz); Andriy Kananovych/Shutterstock Images, front (trilobite); Fokin Oleg/Shutterstock Images, back (granite); Minakryn Ruslan/Shutterstock Images, back (garnet)

Interior Photos: iStockphoto, 1 (top left), 1 (center), 7 (right), 15 (right), 20 (bottom), 24 (top), 27 (bottom), 30, 33, 34 (top), 36 (top), 36 (bottom), 44, 53 (bottom), 54 (top), 56 (top), 56 (bottom), 59 (top), 59 (bottom), 60 (top), 60 (bottom), 61 (top), 64 (top), 68 (top), 68 (bottom), 75 (top), 75 (bottom), 79, 81, 82 (top), 82 (bottom), 87 (top), 88, 89 (top), 90 (top), 90 (bottom), 92, 93, 96 (bottom), 97 (top), 97 (bottom), 98 (bottom), 100, 103, 104 (top), 107 (top), 112 (top left), 112 (top right), 112 (bottom left);

Colin Keates/Dorling Kindersley/Science Source, 1 (top right), 8, 10, 16, 17, 19, 42; Daniel V. Fung/iStockphoto, 1 (bottom left), 62; Shutterstock Images, 1 (bottom right), 9 (left), 9 (right), 22 (right), 26 (bottom), 38, 45, 49, 52 (top), 52 (bottom), 58, 64 (top), 65, 71, 73, 76 (crystals), 85, 91; Minakryn Ruslan/iStockphoto, 4 (left), 5 (copper), 74, 83, 99 (top), 99 (bottom), 107 (bottom); Guillermo Guerao Serra/Shutterstock Images, 4 (middle), 6 (bottom), 14 (bottom); Igor Sokalski/iStockphoto, 4 (right), 105; Red Line Editorial, 5 (infographic); Bjoern Wylezich/Shutterstock Images, 5 (Diplomystus), 24 (bottom); Studio Empreinte/iStockphoto, 5 (obsidian), 53 (top); Krim Kate/iStockphoto, 5 (eclogite), 46, 51 (top), 51 (bottom), 54 (bottom), 57 (top), 66, 67; Bruce Block/iStockphoto, 87 (bottom); Ibe van Oort/Shutterstock Images, 6 (top), 14 (top); S. Leggio/Shutterstock Images, 7 (left), 15 (left); The Natural History Museum, London/Alamy, 11;

ABDOBOOKS.COM

Published by Abdo Publishing, a division of ABDO, PO Box 398166, Minneapolis, Minnesota 55439. Copyright © 2022 by Abdo Consulting Group, Inc. International copyrights reserved in all countries. No part of this book may be reproduced in any form without written permission from the publisher. Abdo Reference™ is a trademark and logo of Abdo Publishing.

102021
012022

Editor: Alyssa Sorenson
Series Designer: Colleen McLaren
Content Consultant: Lars Hansen, PhD, Associate Professor, Department of Earth and Environmental Sciences, University of Minnesota

Library of Congress Control Number: 2021941709

Publisher's Cataloging-in-Publication Data

Names: Lusted, Marcia Amidon, author.
Title: Fossils, rocks, and minerals / by Marcia Amidon Lusted
Description: Minneapolis, Minnesota : Abdo Publishing, 2022 | Series: Field guides | Includes online resources and index.
Identifiers: ISBN 9781532196966 (lib. bdg.) | ISBN 9781098218775 (ebook)
Subjects: LCSH: Fossils--Juvenile literature. | Rocks--Juvenile literature. | Mineralogy--Juvenile literature. | Geology--Juvenile literature. | Field guides--Juvenile literature.
Classification: DDC 550--dc23